BOOK 1

Late Elementary to Early Intermediate

Major Scale **Pro**

Lesson Enhancement Series

Melody Bober | Gayle Kowalchyk | E. L. Lancaster

Foreword

Scales are the foundation of music. Learning to play scales in all keys provides pianists with valuable technical skills: coordinating the hands, learning the keyboard topography of different keys, and increasing speed and agility using basic musical patterns.

Major Scale Pro, Book 1 introduces students to the seven white-key major scales in a systematic way. Basics of building a major scale are presented, first by using tetrachords to learn the pattern of whole steps and half steps. Students then begin to play these scales hands separately for one octave. Practice techniques are given to increase facility, and hands-together playing begins with scales in contrary motion. Finally, students play each scale for one octave, hands together, in contrary and parallel motion with an optional teacher duet. Each one-octave scale is followed by a two-octave scale in the same key, played in parallel and contrary motion, also with an optional teacher duet.

The materials in *Major Scale Pro* will provide a satisfying musical experience as pianists learn important technical skills. When students finish this book, they can move to *Major Scale Pro*, *Book 2*, which introduces the five black-key major scales.

Table of Contents

ISBN-10: 1-4706-2967-4
ISBN-13: 978-1-4706-2967-0
Cover image: Trophy: © Shutterstock.com / sergign

Major Scale Basics

1. What is a major scale?

   A major scale consists of eight notes following a specific sequence of whole and half steps. Each scale begins and ends on the keynote—the note that has the same name as the scale.

2. How can I build a major scale?

   Any major scale can be formed by following this sequence of whole and half steps: W W H W W W H.

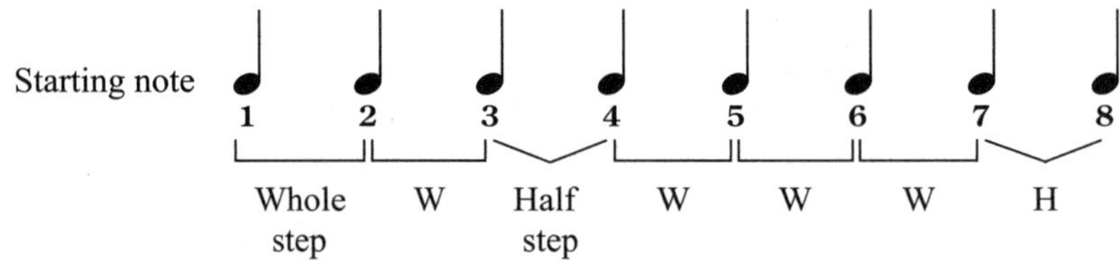

3. What is a tetrachord?

   A tetrachord is a series of four notes: a starting note followed by *whole step, whole step, half step.*

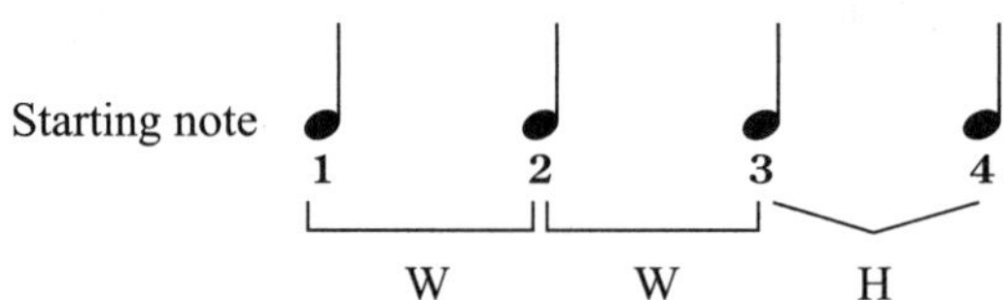

4. How can tetrachords be used to build a major scale?

   Two tetrachords joined by a whole step form a major scale.

5. What is the fingering when playing scales with tetrachords divided between the left hand and right hand?

   Left hand tetrachords are fingered 5 4 3 2.
   Right hand tetrachords are fingered 2 3 4 5.

Building Major Scales Beginning on White Keys

Write letter names on the correct keys for each major scale shown on the staff. Then, play with tetrachord fingering divided between the hands.

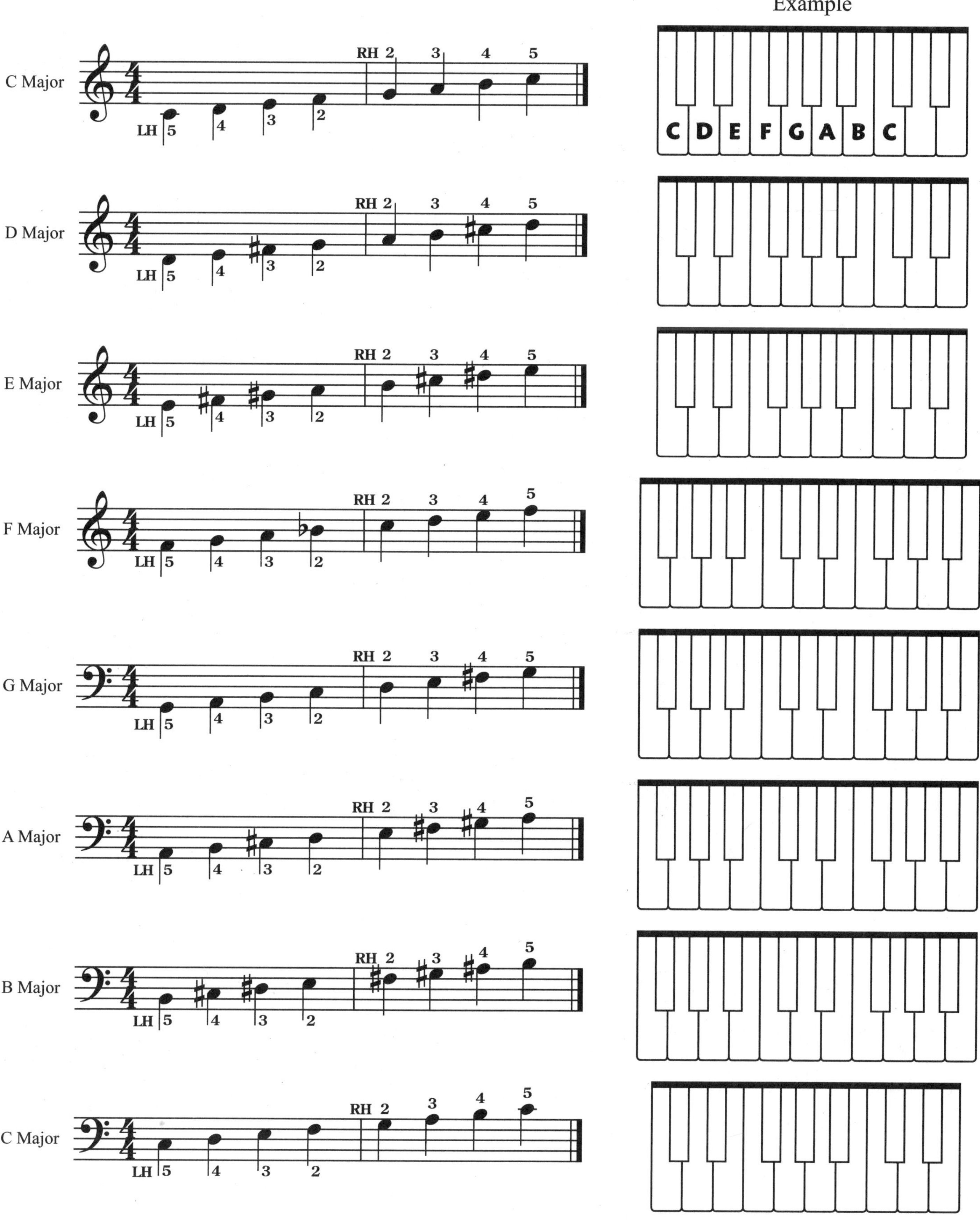

Scale Fingering
(One Octave)

C Major

D Major

E Major

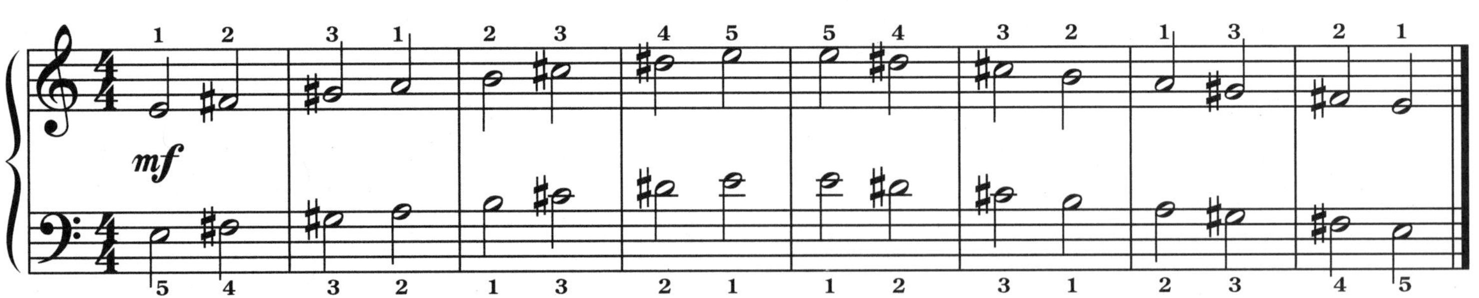

F Major

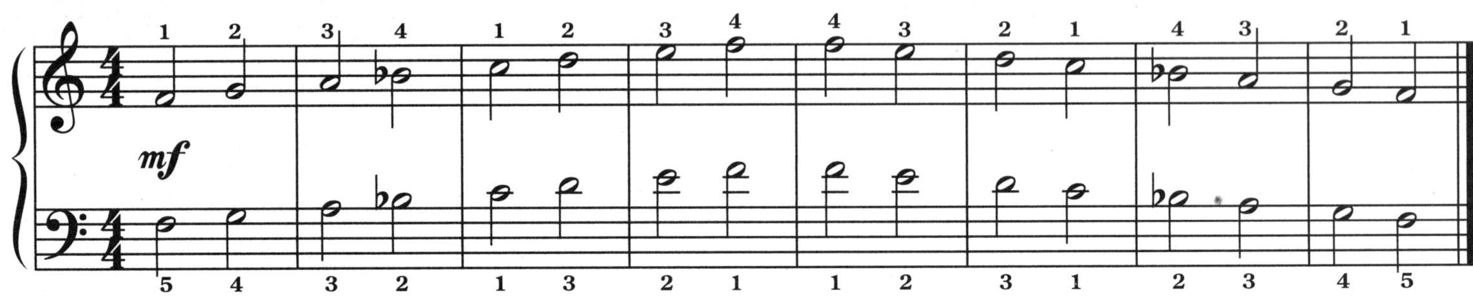

Scale Fingering
(One Octave)

G Major

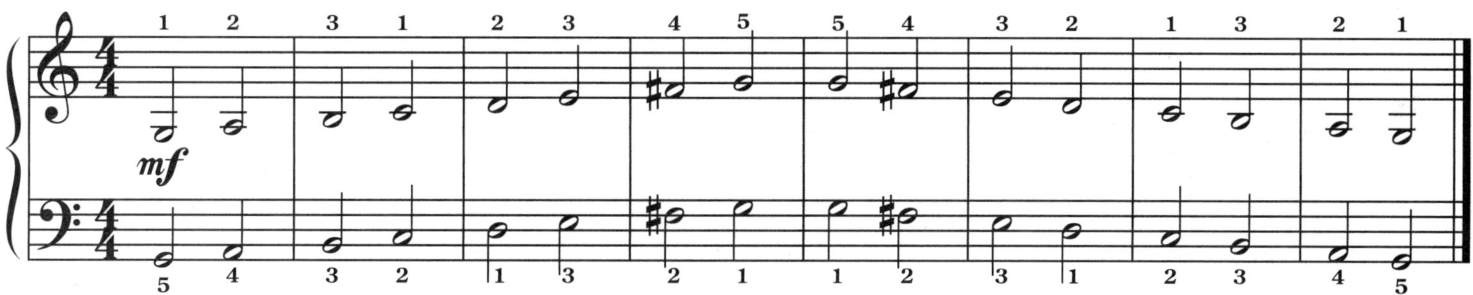

A Major

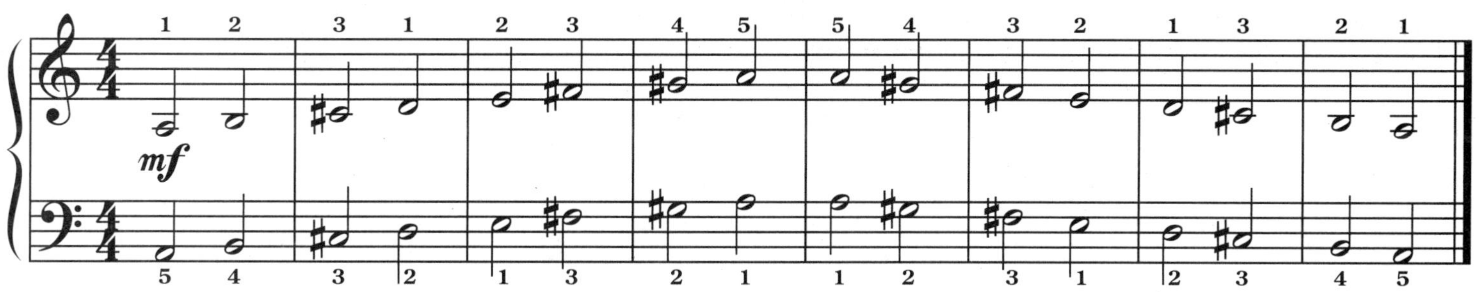

B Major

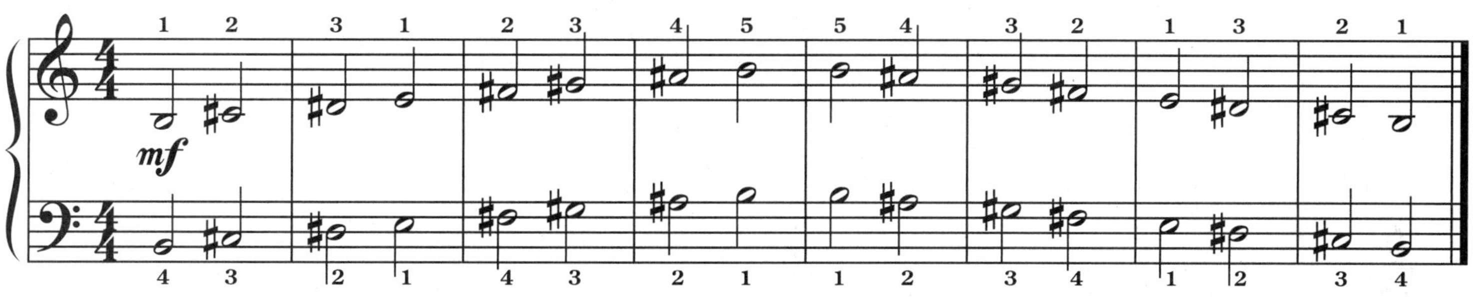

Remembering Scale Fingering

C, D, E, G, and A Major:

1. All five scales use the same fingering.
   One octave RH: 123 12345 LH: 54321 321
   Two octaves RH: 123 1234 123 12345 LH: 54321 321 4321 321
2. The fourth finger plays only once per octave in each scale.
3. When playing hands together, finger 3 in each hand plays at the same time.

F Major:

1. RH: One octave 1234 1234 Two octaves 1234 123 1234 1234
2. LH: Same fingering as C, D, E, G, and A Major
3. When playing hands together, the thumbs play at the same time on F and C (except on the first and last notes).

B Major:

1. RH: Same fingering as C, D, E, G, and A Major
2. LH: One octave 4321 4321 Two octaves 4321 4321 321 4321
3. When playing hands together, the thumbs play at the same time on B and E (except on the first and last notes).

Scale Practice

Practice these exercises to prepare for scale playing.

Scale Practice

Blocking:

Contrary Motion:

F Major

B Major

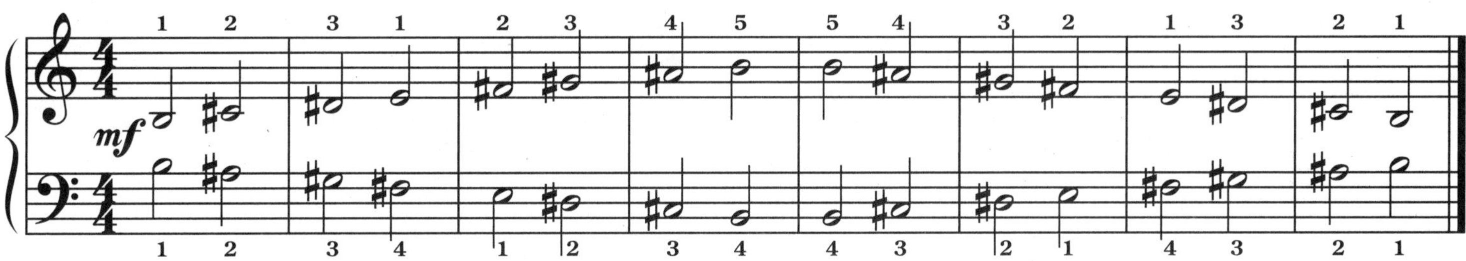

Festival Fun

(One-Octave Scale Duet in C Major)

Melody Bober

Festival Fun

(One-Octave Scale Duet in C Major)

Melody Bober

Festival Divertido

(Two-Octave Scale Duet in C Major)

Melody Bober

Festival Divertido

(Two-Octave Scale Duet in C Major)

Joyously (♩ = 132)

Melody Bober

Both hands one octave higher with duet

Twilight Interlude

(One-Octave Scale Duet in D Major)

Melody Bober

Twilight Interlude

(One-Octave Scale Duet in D Major)

Melody Bober

Moonlight Intermezzo

(Two-Octave Scale Duet in D Major)

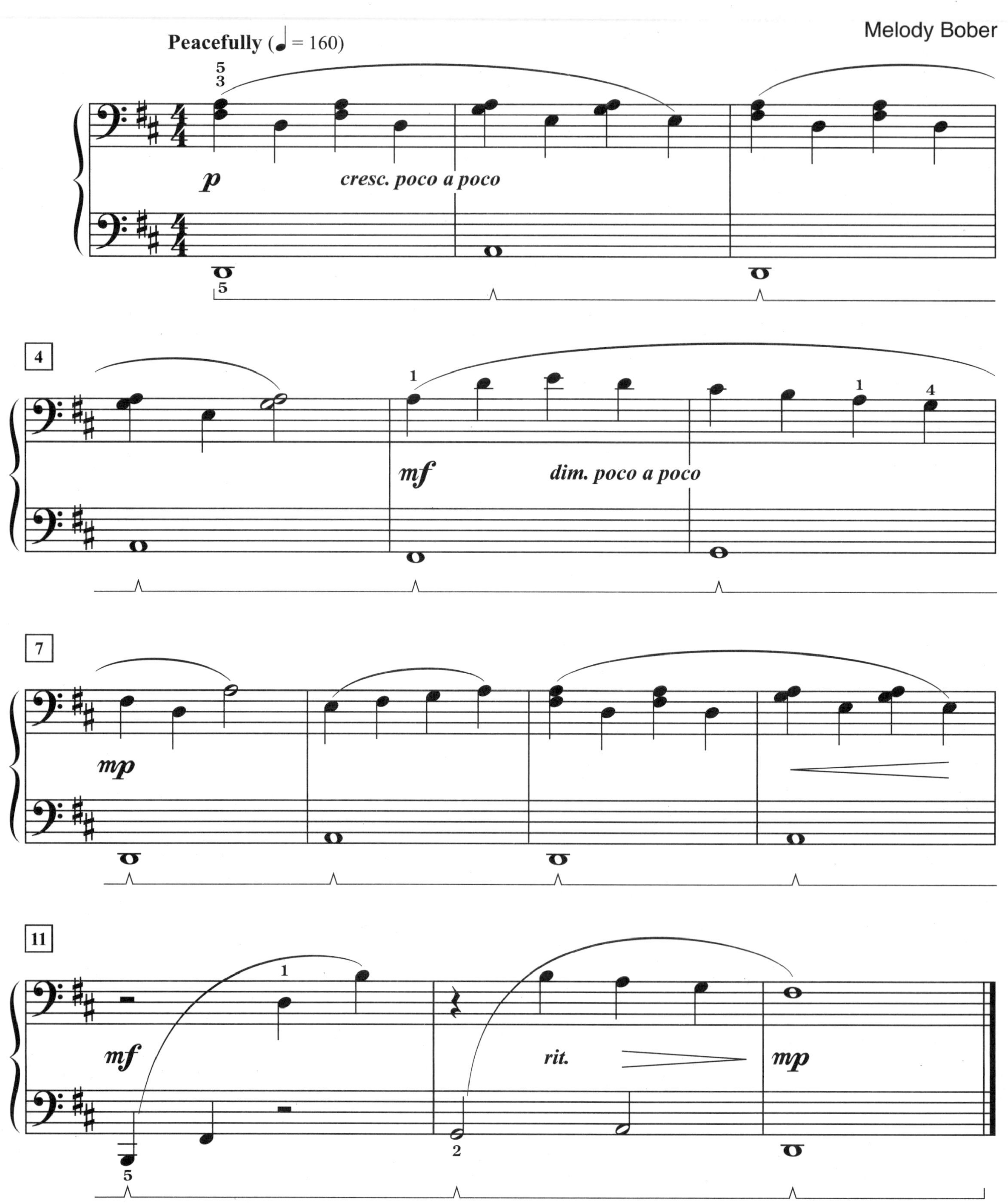

Moonlight Intermezzo

(Two-Octave Scale Duet in D Major)

Melody Bober

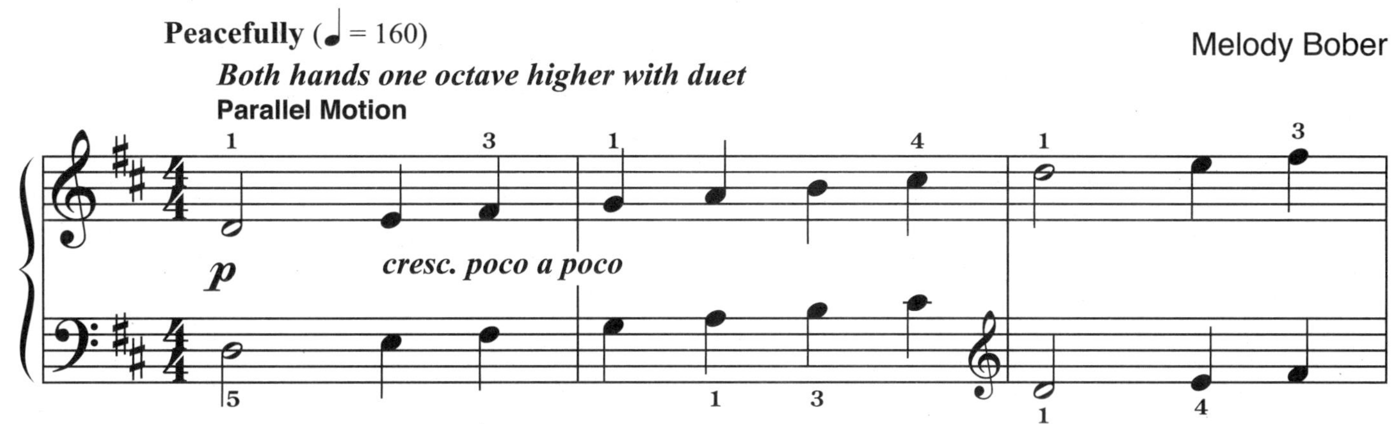

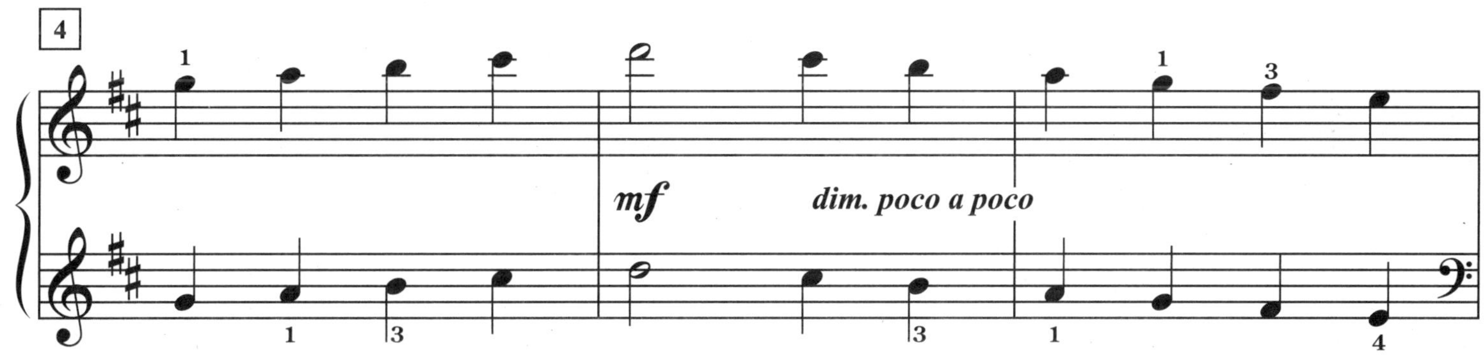

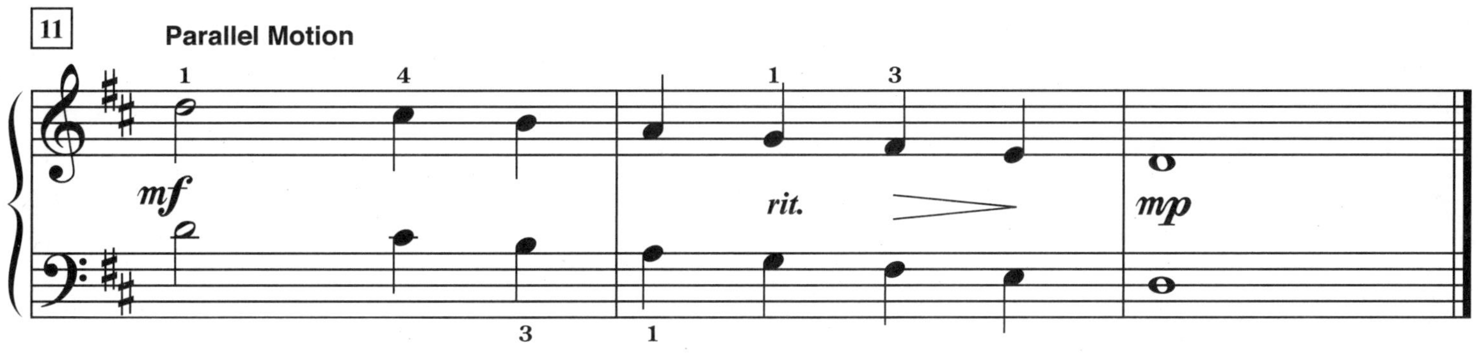

Overture

(One-Octave Scale Duet in E Major)

Melody Bober

Overture

(One-Octave Scale Duet in E Major)

Melody Bober

Reprise

(Two-Octave Scale Duet in E Major)

Melody Bober

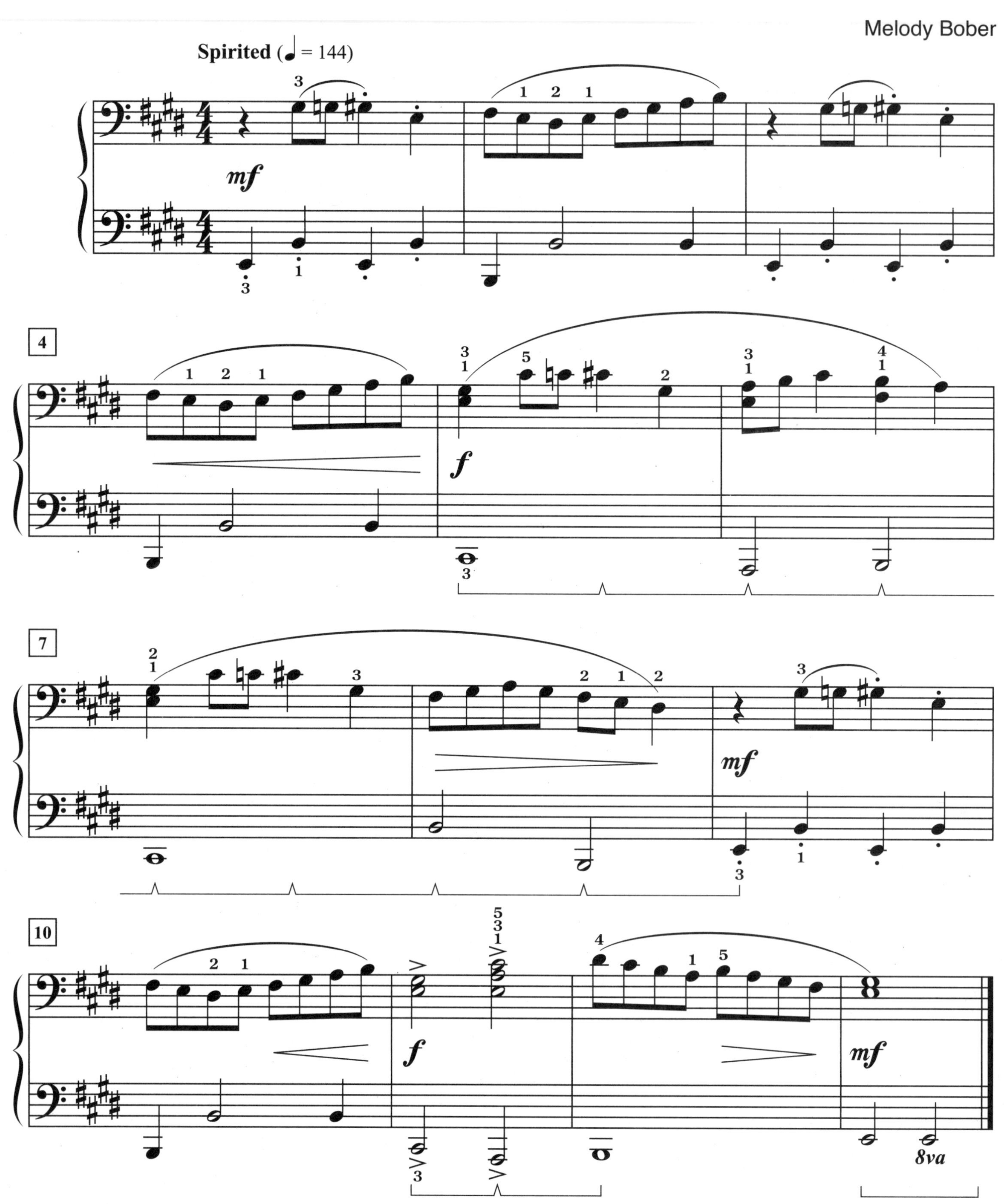

Reprise

(Two-Octave Scale Duet in E Major)

Melody Bober

King of Ragtime

(One-Octave Scale Duet in F Major)

King of Ragtime

(One-Octave Scale Duet in F Major)

Melody Bober

Ode to Scott Joplin

(Two-Octave Scale Duet in F Major)

Melody Bober

Ode to Scott Joplin

(Two-Octave Scale Duet in F Major)

Melody Bober

Jazz Lights

(One-Octave Scale Duet in G Major)

Melody Bober

Jazz Lights

(One-Octave Scale Duet in G Major)

Melody Bober

Jazzy Nights

(Two-Octave Scale Duet in G Major)

Melody Bober

Jazzy Nights

(Two-Octave Scale Duet in G Major)

Melody Bober

Kickin' Country

(One-Octave Scale Duet in A Major)

Melody Bober

Kickin' Country

(One-Octave Scale Duet in A Major)

Melody Bober

Boots 'n' Spurs

(Two-Octave Scale Duet in A Major)

Melody Bober

Boots 'n' Spurs

(Two-Octave Scale Duet in A Major)

Melody Bober

Celtic Charm

(One-Octave Scale Duet in B Major)

Melody Bober

Celtic Charm

(One-Octave Scale Duet in B Major)

Melody Bober

Ireland Forever

(Two-Octave Scale Duet in B Major)

Melody Bober

Ireland Forever

(Two-Octave Scale Duet in B Major)

Practice Challenge

Transpose to D, E, F, G, A, and B Major